IMAGES
of England

Around
TOTNES

IMAGES
of England

AROUND TOTNES

Totnes Image Bank

TEMPUS

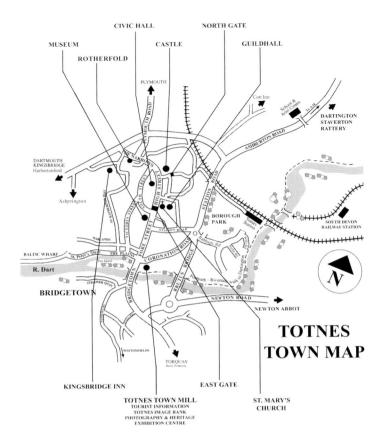

TOTNES TOWN MAP

Frontispiece: Arthur Benjamin Niner. Town Crier and Bill Poster, 1890s.

First published 2002, reprinted 2003

Tempus Publishing Limited
The Mill, Brimscombe Port,
Stroud, Gloucestershire, GL5 2QG

British Library Cataloguing in Publication Data.
A catalogue record for this book is available from the British Library.

ISBN 0 7524 2648 6

Typesetting and origination by Tempus Publishing Limited
Printed in Great Britain by Midway Colour Print, Wiltshire.

Contents

The High Street before 1878. This picture can be dated as the clock in the East Gate was installed by public subscription in 1878. This photograph is a copy of the original, believed to be a Daguerrotype.

Introduction

A Little History

Walk around the town of Totnes and you will see a visible history; stone and timber framed buildings, the castle, ancient walkways, wells and springs. They represent over 1,000 years of living history, from the time when the Saxons established a defensive fort on a strategic bend in the river Dart and the invading Normans developed the town of Totnes from 1086, and the corresponding expansion of the town's layout to become much as we see it today, with the castle dominating the skyline.

The evidence of how people lived in those early days is very sketchy. Documents and clothing nearly always decay and only objects like the silver coins minted by Judael the Norman Lord of Totnes survive because of the metals that they are made of. As time moves on towards the present day more physical evidence survives. The Totnes Elizabethan Museum is a fine example of a Tudor merchant's house of the 1500s, and the foundations of the Guildhall date back to the days of the Priory and Norman times.

Until the invention of photography in around 1850 we relied on the artist to record the visual scene and the writer to convey the mental image of places and events. With the sudden explosion of the industrial revolution, science and technology accelerated the development of travel, mechanisation and communications. At the same time the new discoveries in science made photography a practical reality. In England in 1840 Fox Talbot invented the Calotype paper negative process and in France, a year earlier, Louis Daguerre patents his Daguerreotype camera, which produced a one-off picture on a metal plate. Before the end of the 1800s photographers were recording scenes of everyday life at home and abroad. It is this fragile photographic evidence which it is so important to gather together from various sources and combine in an archive of visual history of the town of Totnes.

Around Totnes and The Totnes Image Bank

The contents of this book represent a small selection of photographs from the Totnes Image Bank, a photographic archive covering many subjects from the beginnings of photography to the present day. We are encouraging photographers to record today's events so that future generations will see how the town of Totnes lived, changed and developed in the twenty-first century.

The Totnes Image Bank is a charitable trust. It came into being when in 1998 Nicholas and Fay Horne, retired Totnes photographers, entrusted me with their collection of photographs. I had been wondering what to do with my own collection of photographic work, and when the responsibility of the Hornes' work came along the decision was made for me. With a group of like-minded individuals a Trust was formed with a specific object – 'to save and protect the photographic heritage of Totnes and the surrounding area for the educational benefit of the public'.

The collection grew again when Eric Morison's family donated his work, all in negatives and plates. This represented another High Street photographer's view of the town. Rosemary Westell, a keen amateur photographer working from the 1970s to the present day, gave us her negative collection of people and places in and around the town, along with her father's work taken in the 1930s and 1940s.

South Hams newspapers donated over thirty years of negatives covering the South Hams area, and many other smaller contributors have either donated or loaned pictures for scanning into our computer database. The total number of negatives, plates, transparencies and prints now adds up to around 600,000 items. All this material is slowly being catalogued and scanned by a team of volunteers. What you see in this book is the first selection from 3,000 images that have been scanned into our computer database.

Finding detailed information to accompany the photographs can sometimes be very difficult. If you have any further information that would add to the history and background of any of the pictures in the book please contact us (details of our address, web-site etc. are on the back page).

The photographs in this book are not individually credited (please see the acknowledgements section at the end of the book); we have not knowingly or deliberately reproduced any photographs that are not the copyright of the Totnes Image Bank or without the owner's permission.

We are always on the lookout for more images of Totnes, the river and the surrounding area to broaden our view of the town and the overall picture that is created through photography. If you have any local pictures, whatever the subject, and you would like to share these images through the Totnes Image Bank project please let us know. Original pictures are scanned into the computer database and returned to the contributor. It is the Totnes Image Bank Trust policy to make as many of the archive's images available to the public as possible. This book represents a selection of images in print. Exhibitions of original prints can be seen in Totnes at various venues during the year and a permanent exhibition of photography is always on show at the Image Bank's HQ at Town Mill, Totnes. All this material and much more is on view through our computer database in Town Mill. If you like any particular image that you see in this book or on our database you can purchase high quality photographic prints.

The trustees and the volunteers at the Totnes Image Bank hope you enjoy our first selection of *Around Totnes*.

Barrington Weekes
Trustee & Project Manager

Foreword

'*Unanimity and prosperity to the town of Totnes and success to the trade thereof,*' the town motto and an indication of its history and vibrancy. The tidal head of the river Dart made it an ideal place to ship tin and wool down the river to Dartmouth and beyond. It is a meeting place for, and home to, many wealthy merchants.

To understand the topography and its effect on the lives of those who lived and worked in and around the town in those early days before the invention of photography, we have to rely on the artists, poets, playwrights and authors of the time. Unfortunately we have to allow for poetic license, and cannot therefore always be too sure that their work is a true representation of the place and its people.

With the coming of photography and latterly the new technology, it is now possible to accurately record, store and display all the pictorial evidence that we need to surf the town's important buildings, events and the characters who played their part in its ongoing history.

The East Gate fire in 1990 made us realise how important it was to have a permanent record of the past. Thanks to the details held, the nationally recognised Arch has long since been restored to its former glory. Preserving and enhancing the historic core of the town and its environmental setting and maintaining the financial viability of its shops and businesses is a challenge. Equally challenging is the recording of what we have, what happened and who made the news during this and the last millennium. The Image Bank will enable this to happen, taking Totnes back to the future and forward to the past.

Judy Westacott
Mayor, 2002/03

One
High Street and Above

Totnes Castle from the North Gate, Castle Street, taken in 1986. This fine Norman motte and bailey castle, built in 1086 by Judhael of Totnes, is now under the protection of English Heritage.

Parts of the Guildhall date back to 1088. It continued to be used as a court until 1974.

Totnes Voluntary Primary church school, mixed class 1906. The school was built in 1866.

Totnes Voluntary primary church school. Girls class 1906.

Corn Exchange, also known as Church Walk in the High Street, erected in 1611. Some of the pillars now stand outside the Guildhall.

Church Walk on the High Street, demolished in 1878, showing the East Gate before the clock was installed.

No. 54 High Street, a branch of Lloyds bank, pictured in about 1960.

No. 58a International Stores in the High Street with goods displayed in the windows, around 1960.

No. 93 High Street, Nicholas Horne, photographers, *c*. 1960.

No. 58 High Street, Reeves Stores,
Ironmongers, in around 1960.

Left: An early photograph of St Mary's church, built in the fifteenth century and made of local red sandstone, here pictured in around 1900. *Right:* Compare the two photographs, there are many changes to the building and churchyard, *c.* 1950.

Church Close before the buildings on the right were demolished, photographed here in around 1900.

Butterwalk on the left in the High Street, around 1900. Water from Harper's Well was stored in conduits at the Market Place, opposite No. 52 High Street.

 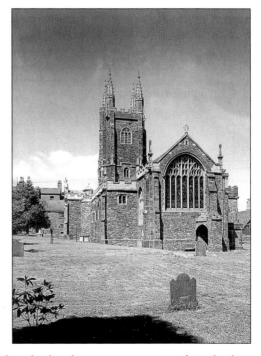

Left: St Mary's church. *Right:* The churchyard after the headstones were removed in the late 1950s.

Entrance to F.T. Tucker's sweet factory in the early 1900s. Now it is the entrance to Castle Court residential housing.

Looking up the High Street to the Castle Hotel, 1920. The Butterwalk on the right, it was here that the 'hose of fine Totnes' was sold, Totnes being one of the chief clothing marts of the kingdom.

High Street in the 1960s. Note the police telephone box next to the public call box.

No. 11 High Street, Totnes. The shop front was extensively 'modernised' during rebuilding in 1935, and was converted for Millbay Laundry.

Rooftops of the old market building in the 1930s. The Market Hall, of 1594, was replaced in 1848. Stalls were moved from the High Street pavements to covered lock-ups surrounding the Market Hall.

The Narrows, a policeman waiting to direct two-way traffic, *c.* 1940.

Coalman delivering in the Rotherfold, *c.* 1940. Coal was only delivered by the coalman, if coke was required it had to be fetched from the Gasworks at The Grove.

Smokey Totnes from the Castle ramparts, c. 1930.

No. 6 North Street in the 1930s. It is now called Pound House.

Washday in one of the passages off the
High Street, c. 1930.

The Rotherfold in the 1940s, looking down The Narrows. The horse and cart belong to Mr
Skedgell, a coal merchant.

Two-way traffic passing through The Narrows. The Plymouth Inn is on the left, *c.* 1920.

Traffic in the 1920s with Skewis & Co, the Post Office, 93 High Street.

The seventeenth-century Kingsbridge Inn in around the 1880s. Solicitor Thomas Creaser Kellock is walking from his house, Highfield. Local photographer Joseph Brinley is on the left. The building opposite the inn known as Steps Cottage was the old lookout tower.

The Dart Vale Hunt meet at the Kingsbridge Inn. Mrs K. Jones is with a drinks tray and Graham Knowles, whipper-in of the hunt, is in the centre foreground, c. 1950.

Northgate, *c.* 1930, the postman and delivery boys. The one on the right is Maurice Henry Kelland Clements, who worked for Ekers the fishmongers. The house on the right has been demolished to widen North Street.

Two

Fore Street
and the Plains

The old bridge across the river Dart was narrow, with V-shaped recesses in the roadway. The foundations of this old bridge, which was on the north side of the present bridge, may still be seen at low water. The illustration is from around 1820.

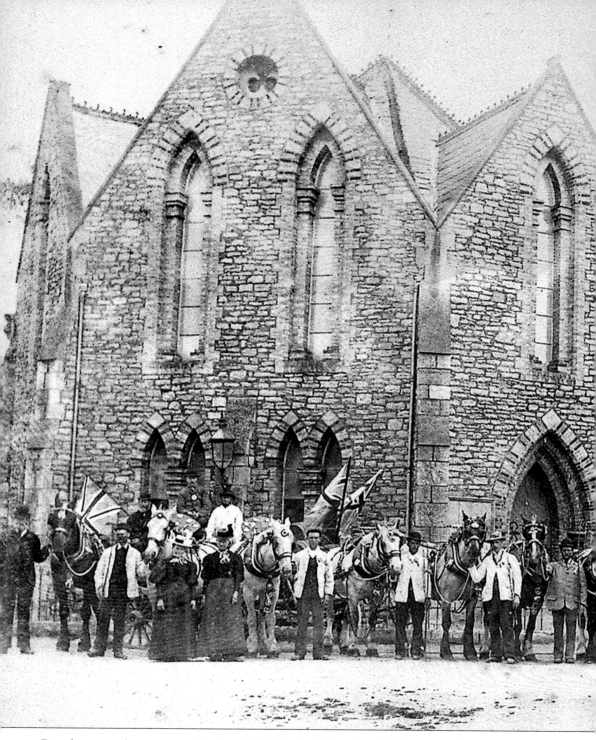

Dray horses and grooms outside the old Methodist Chapel on the Plains in about 1890. There are now residential flats here.

East Gate, Fore Street, *c.* 2000. The East Gate, known locally as the Arch, separates High Street from Fore Street.

East Gate, Fore Street, *c.* 1900. The walls of the archway probably date back to 1265, Henry III granting liberty to enclose the town with a wall for collecting taxes. Originally the archway enclosed gates large enough to admit traffic with a needle's eye for people on foot.

Two-way traffic in Fore Street with a policeman on point duty at the junction of Station Road, c. 1930.

The road mender outside Nos 58-60 Fore Street.

The Mansion, late eighteenth century, was the King Edward V1 Grammar school and is currently in use for further education. Photograph taken in the 1940s.

Portland House photographed in 1935. This building was next to the Royal Seven Stars Hotel and was demolished to make way for Coronation Road in 1937.

Under the East Gate Arch looking down Fore Street in 1961.

Looking down Fore Street to the Plains around the time of the Horse Sales.

The late eighteenth century Gothic house has a public right of way running through it. This picture was taken in 1953.

Hatchet's at 47 Fore Street, a brick, mid-Georgian house with a Venetian window. Photographed after the building had been restored in the 1980s.

The Dartmouth Inn in 1979 and before restoration of this area.

The Town Mill about 1902 with miller, William Cole. This building is now the Totnes Tourist Information Centre and the Totnes Image Bank HQ.

Harris Bacon Factory, originally built as a granary in the Crimean War. The business moved to these premises in 1912, drawing pigs from local farms from Devon and East Cornwall. It closed in the 1980s. The site has now been redeveloped by Safeway.

The millers Cole outside the Town Mill, 1902. The Town Mill dating back to 1588 once had two water wheels sited each side to provide power.

Donkey Delivery
Service 1900 style.
Photograph taken at
the Grammar school.

Elaborate decorations at the end of the Plains for Queen Victoria's Jubilee in 1897. The Mayor's
house had an arch of three spans stretching across the road to his warehouses opposite.

Horse Sales taking place on the Plains, *c.* 1900.

The monument to William Wills stands opposite his home on the Plains and commemorates his expedition to cross Australia in 1860.

Cars neatly parked in the centre of the Plains in the 1940s.

Before the restoration of Totnes Waterside from the Plains in 1982.

Parade on the Plains. Rendle Crang is leading the first group, John Pascoe the next.

Holman's, grain merchants, warehouses on the Plains. They sold a diverse range of agricultural products, such as oil and coke, corn, seed, grains, manure, hay and straw.

Empty warehouses on the Plains in 1979. These once impressive buildings and an ealier Brew or Malt House stood on what was known as Marsh Quay. Now they have been converted into flats overlooking the Mill Tail.

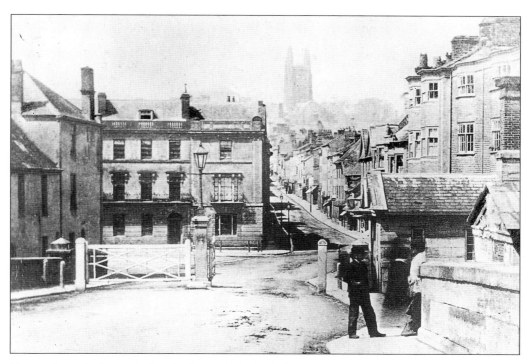

Totnes from the New Bridge, built in 1826-1828; the toll gates were removed in 1881.

Bridgetown in the nineteenth century, showing the Seymour Hotel and Bridgetown church, both built by the eleventh Duke of Somerset.

View of Bridgetown from St John's church tower, 1968, looking towards Totnes.

Tanyard Marsh and lower Bridgetown, before housing development, 1981.

Bridgetown has gradually lost its shops, becoming a residential area with a few businesses. A film company recreated the street scene depicting the 1950s era. Houses became shops again just for a day.

Three
River Dart

On the river in 1919. Sharpham Boathouse is surrounded by dense foliage of trees in the background. C. Binmore is on the left.

Left: Sailing ship at St Peters Quay, 1865. For centuries the river Dart has been the trading link between Totnes and the outside world. Before the advent of the railway large cargoes arrived by sea. The roads in Britain were so bad that regular deliveries of large cargoes would have been impossible.

Below: Ecklolm unloading timber for F.J. Reeves in the Mill Tail, 1903. The first timber ships were sailing boats, then steam ships and finally modern cargo boats, carrying 1,000 tons of timber at a time.

During the Second World War, sixteen 105ft Motor Minesweepers and seven 125ft types were built at Totnes, all of them wooden vessels. After the hulls were launched they were brought to the quay for completion of all the upper works and the fitting out.

600 workers were employed on minesweeper production at peak period. Work at Totnes started in 1940 under the direction of Frank Curtis Ltd, Cornwall, with local unskilled labour. Included in the group are Mr Syms, Mr Higgs, Bill Westaway, Ned Syms and Percy Tidball.

Aerial view of the River Dart, 1964. On the left-hand side of the river Dart can be seen the unloading quays and timber sheds of F.J. Reeves Ltd. With a work force of 240 people and ships

delivering timber from Poland, Russia, Finland and Sweden this company contributed significantly to the economy of the town.

The Paddle Steamer, Compton Castle, at Steamer Quay. These pleasure boats operate between Totnes and Dartmouth.

Paddle Steamer leaving Steamer Quay for Dartmouth. The steamer service began in 1836.

Steamer Quay slipway 1931. Pleasure boats, *Dart, Sons of the Dart, Theodora* and *Sunmaid* operated by Ned Syms, Bill Allen and Perce Williams.

Totnes Castle approaching Totnes, 1961. Honnor Marine boat sheds can be seen on the river bank. This steamer was built by Philips at Dartmouth in 1923.

Three timber ships after discharging their cargoes of timber at Baltic Wharf in the early 1960s.

Left: Minesweepers were constructed in this shed. F.J. Reeves used this building until it was replaced by a modern construction in the 1980s. *Right:* The F.J. Reeves replacement building was used as a timber machine shop, late 1980s.

The Elm turning on its way to Dartmouth and beyond, 1990s. The River Commissioners and F.J. Reeves constructed this turning bay for the longer ships to manoeuvre in the 1970s.

Unloading packets of timber from the *Astrid Bres* onto Baltic Wharf, 1986.

The Mill Tail, Vire Island and the river Dart, 1960. The Island first opened as a pleasure park in 1844 and was renamed Vire Island in 1978 for the Normandy town twinned with Totnes.

Timber boats unloading at St Peters Quay. The track of the old Quay Line on the left was opened in 1873 and was in use until 1966.

Bres Line captains, Per Bredevang and Mogens Iversen (left) on the bridge of the *Astrid Bres*. 1986. Mogans was mate on the first Bres Line ship to come from Denmark in 1961. Twenty-five years later he was captain of the *Astrid Bres* arriving in the Dart to celebrate the twenty-fifth anniversary of Bres Line and F. J. Reeves collaboration of importing timber into Totnes.

Astrid Bres on the Dart at Duncannon on the twenty-fifth anniversary of timber trading between Bres Line and F.J. Reeves. The river pilot was David Griffiths.

Timber arriving at high water on an icy winters morning.

The *Ulla Danya* turning in the river Dart after unloading timber in the Mill Tail, 1970s.

Fiona on her bottom in the Mill Tail, 1960s.

The dredger *Panurgic* in 1988. Believed to be the last time the river Dart was dredged at Totnes.

Astrid Bres leaving Totnes 1986.

Four

People and Events

George Windeatt, Town Clerk in the 1950s.

Left: Edmund B. Stoyle, Mayor in 1922. He was an outfitter and lived at 34 High Street.
Right: Jeffrey Michelmore, Mayor in 1874/75 and '79. Land and estate agent at Gate House, East Gate, High Street, and who lived at Pomeroy House, Bridgetown.

Left: Henry Symons, JP and Mayor, 1886. Symons business was on the Plains and he lived at Tuckenhay.
Right: Charles Frederick Rae BA. BSc. Mayor, 1916 to 1918. Headmaster at Totnes Grammar school 1896 to 1915.

Mr G. Reginald Perrow, Mayor 1958, with Deputy Mayor, town clerk, mace bearer and town sergeants in the Guildhall.

Mayor choosing, 1946. The first Lady Mayor of Totnes, Mrs Lilian Ramsden.

Mayor choosing 1970, Mrs Jean Gilbert. This event still takes place in the Guildhall each May. The roll of Mayors dates back to 1359.

Lewis Major, Mayor, leading a procession on the opening of the 1985 Elizabethan Season in the High Street.

Totnes Elizabethans in the High Street, 1970. Totnes Elizabethan Day started in 1970 during the summer season when shopkeepers and locals dressed in costume. Tuesday was chosen as it was a quiet trading day.

Old-fashioned transport in the Rotherfold, 1980s.

Harry and Kathleen Thomas, Totnes
Elizabethans, 1984.

The Gentleman's Club, 1920s. The group includes Sidney Leonard, Jack Leonard, Mr Salter, Alfred Leonard, Mr Murch, Ernie Hawke and Alfred Syms.

Totnes Bowling Club in the Borough Park in front of the Bandstand.

St Mary's church choir outing, 1920s.

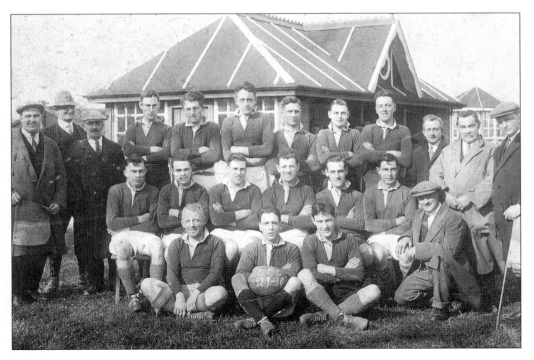

Totnes Rugby Football Club, 1929, in the Borough Park.

Totnes Rugby Football Team 1898/99. In order from the back row, left to right: C. Hooper, E. Knott, H. Tucker, J. Veale, S. Kinsman, (Capt) G.E. Windeatt, W. Tozer, W. Hawkins,

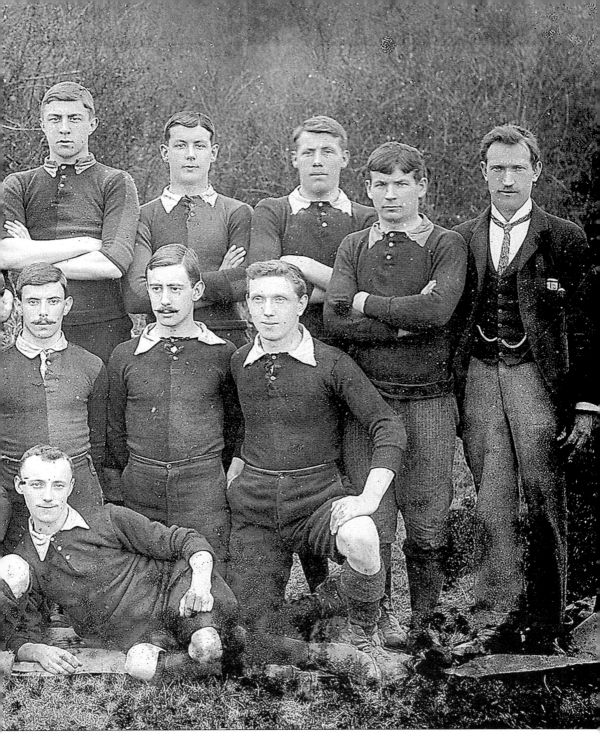

G. Scoble, F. Kinsman, E. Adams, P.E. Adams, J. Windeatt, H.B. Tucker, Frank Kinsman, R. Elias, L. Stoyle and S.E. Rodgers.

Her Majesty the Queen and the Duke of Edinburgh in the Guildhall with Mayor Douglas Mitchell on her visit in 1962.

Her Majesty the Queen outside St Mary's church in 1962. Her Majesty was the first reigning monarch to visit the borough since 1625.

Queen's Jubilee Celebrations, 1977, at Brooklands.

Queen's Jubilee Party 1977 at Leechwell Mews with Mayor Mr William Bennett.

At the grindstone, *c.* 1930.

Beating the Bounds with the Mayor, 1905.

78

Harvest Festival Dinner at the old Civic Hall, 1953. Presiding at the top table were Mr Ernest Nott, Mayor, and the Revd Gordon Samuel.

News-vendor on the corner of the Plains, 1980.

Unveiling of the War Memorial, June 1921, by Lt Col. F.B. Mildmay MP. Mayor Benjamin Hayman is flanked by Mace Bearers. The granite memorial was designed by Sir Reginald Blomfield.

No1 Platoon 'D' Coy thirteenth Devons Home Guard, 1940s, taken at Redworth school. In the group were Bill Harris, Gus Libby, Harold Farr, Bill Clarke, Dick Bolt, Norman Emmett.

Bridgetown Housing Project built at lower Westonfields and named Pathfields in 1946. Lilian Ramsden, Mayor, laid the first brick.

Totnes Times staff, Bill Baker and Norman Emmett in the 1940s. *The Totnes Times* newspaper was established in 1860 with offices at 34 Fore Street; the print workshop was behind with an entrance from Victoria Street. The newspaper came out on a Friday and newsagents came to fetch their own papers for sale that morning.

The Carnival Queen's galleon leading the procession in the 1950s. The galleon was built by Staverton Contractors and it was used for several years. The Queen was Ann Williams and one of her attendants was June Prowse. Percy Turle from Ashburton designed the float.

Scout group behind Bogan House in 1941.

Five

Fire

Totnes firemen at the fire station, built in 1899 as part of the market building. Front row, left to right: Supt Jeffery, -?-, Tom Timewell, Will Hooppell, Fred seaford, Tommy Egerton, Frank Southcott, Tom Heath, Bert Hooppell, Bill Smith. Back Row: Bill Seaford, Harry Distin, Fred Horn, -?-, Bob Reed.

Firemen at practise at the Racecourse with the new steam fire engine *Gem of Totnes*, purchased in 1899 together with 1100 ft of hose. A properly organised voluntary brigade was formed in Totnes in 1877 and local insurance companies were invited to contibute towards the costs.

A Merryweather motor fire engine was purchased in 1929 with full equipment costing £1000 and was christened *The Dart* on 5 July 1929. Back row, left to right: B. Hooppell, W. Hawkins, T. Perring, J. Owen, J. Binden, W Seaford, A Rumbelow (driver), W. Jordan. Front Row: T Timewell (sub. captain), E. Hodge, W. Hooppell, P. Yeoman, W Davies (surveyor), W. Howis (chairman), R. Hooppell (captain).

Fire engine in The Narrows used for the wedding of Iris and Thomas Perring in 1943.

A very casual approach from the public to a disastrous fire that burnt down the Civic Hall and market area in the centre of the town in 1955.

Street scene of the Civic Hall fire, 1955. Part of the Market Hall was coverted to a public hall (now the Civic Hall) with stage and seating in 1948, until destroyed by fire.

Tonight's hypnotic performance will have to be cancelled owing to unforeseen circumstances!

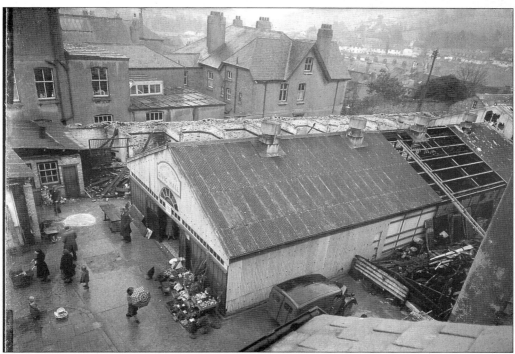

The fire damage to the Civic Hall and the market stalls was attributed to a boiler failure at the rear of the hall.

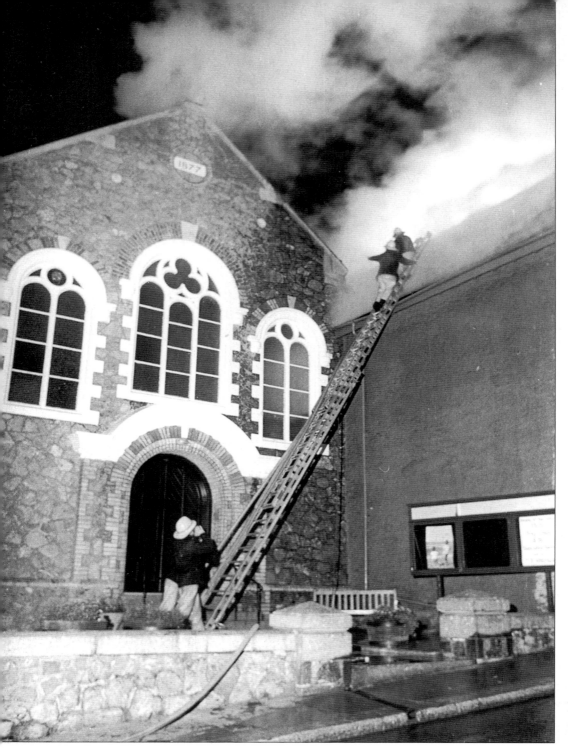

Fore Street, 1987. The United Reform church erected in 1877 was the scene of firemen working to halt the spread of a fire that had started in an empty premises next door.

58-60 Fore Street, night fire, 1987. The photographer got a soaking from the water cascading off the roof of the building.

Lorry fire on Brutus Bridge, March 1986.

A group of firemen at the new fire station in Station Road,1964.

Fire on the Plains, around midnight, January 1986. The fire destroyed the Women's Centre at No. 4 the Plains.

Aftermath of the fire. Demolition of the Women's Centre, watched by Antony Sumner and Sue Harker.

Nos 6 and 7 the Plains. A destructive blaze fanned by strong winds tore through this recently restored Georgian building in 1989. Fearful of the shopping arcade's collapse, firemen were withdrawn. Many shops, flats and offices were destroyed or demolished and have since been rebuilt.

Fire in F.J. Reeves' timber processing plant at Warland, 1989. This company ceased trading in the 1980s and the site has now become housing.

F.J. Reeves' fire, showing the Warland street scene and the old Reeves' Social Club, 1989.

The Great Fire of Totnes, 500 years of history going up in flames. Photographed early in the morning of 4 September 1990. Firemen from the local station were on the scene in minutes shortly after the fire broke out at midnight and managed to get the fire under control by daybreak.

After the fire the road was closed for many months. The final bill for rebuilding was estimated at ten million. The reconstruction work eventually began almost a year after this fire, and was completed by 1992.

Opposite: The fire started in a building on the right of the East Gate Arch, spreading through the arch to buildings on the other side of the road. The cause of the fire being put down, possibly, to faulty wiring in an office of a building owned by the Duke of Somerset.

Following Page: Looking from South Street, the East Gate is on the left and Courtney Blake's house blazes out of control.

Six

Transport

Plymouth bound train, leaving Totnes Station. Note the siding on the left and the semaphore signalling in 1980.

Engine No.1466, 'Bulliver', the Ashburton branch line train approaching Totnes down line platform, 1959.

Double header express train. The leading engine is a Castle class passing through Totnes Station towards Newton Abbot.

Charlie Fennamore, signalman, on duty in Totnes Signal Box, 1980. The box was built in 1923, closed in 1987 and became a café in 1992.

Climbing away from Totnes towards Plymouth at Lee Mill, 1959.

An early diesel hauled passenger train at Lee Mill, 1959.

A British Rail engine waiting to shunt two 'Victoria coaches' onto the Dart Valley Railway branch line, 1981.

Her Majesty the Queen and the Duke of Edinburgh arrive at Totnes Station on their way to Dartmouth, 1988.

The cast-iron footbridge spanning four rail tracks, dated 1888. In 1847 the railroad reached Totnes on the main route from Newton Abbot to Plymouth.

The footbridge was damaged by a British Rail track crane during weekend maintenance work, 1987.

The damaged bridge is cut free.

Footbridge finally removed.

The Royal Train at Totnes Station, 1986.

Prince Charles at Totnes Station, 1986.

Anderton & Rolands' fairground traction engine stuck below the East Gate Arch.

Out of control, a traction engine with a load of timber slides on the wet road in Fore Street.

Symons Cyder Store on the Plains, 1950s. The business began in 1815 (possibly started in Tuckenhay) and closed in 1958 when it relocated to Somerset. These warehouses have since been redeveloped by the Totnes and District Preservation Trust into business and housing premises.

Car crash outside Harrisons Garage on Totnes Bridge, 1927. This business was started by Charles Henry Niles and Charles Ashley Harrison in 1913. They originally traded from the mews behind the Royal Seven Stars Hotel. In 1998 the garage relocated to purpose built premises on the industrial estate, the building was demolished and replaced by flats.

Rail trucks were a familiar site on the Plains up until the late 1950s. Locomotives were not permitted to cross the main road from the branch line. Clydesdale horses were kept in stables by the Blight family for the purpose of moving wagons from St Peters Quay along the Plains and across the road beside Harrisons Garage. This view shows the last day of horse-drawn operation, 31 May 1948. The two men leading the horses are Bill Phillips and George Luscombe.

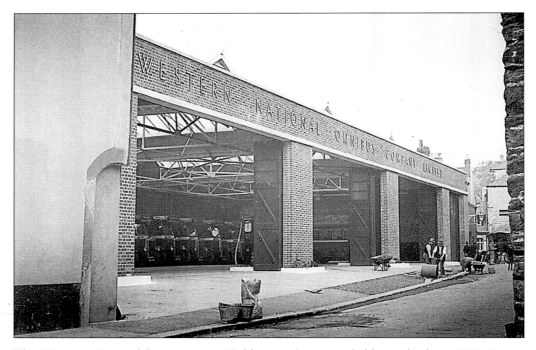

The Western National bus garage in Ticklemore Street, probably in the late 1930s. It was replaced by residential flats in the 1980s.

A rare site of a vintage car travelling down the High Street before the one-way traffic system.

Seven
Villages

Harberton Church House Inn and church, *c.* 1950.

Berry Pomeroy church, *c.* 1950 The photograph is taken from the vicarage drive. The church of St Mary dates back to the fifteenth century and is perpendicular in style with a fine arch and tower. The church was rebuilt by the Pomeroy family and bears their arms on the vaulted roof.

Berry Pomeroy church porch, *c.* 1950.

Berry Pomeroy from the church tower, showing Berry Barton Farm, now Berry Farm, 1987.

Berry Pomeroy from the church tower shows the churchyard and the vicarage, 1987.

Berry Pomeroy looking towards the school, 1987.

Berry Pomeroy Castle, c. 1950. There has been a castle on this site since the Norman Conquest. The present castle was rebuilt in the fourteenth century.

Aerial photograph of Dartington Hall; the Great Hall is in the centre of the picture and the theatre and music schools are on the left.

The Devon Vale Hunt at the Cott Inn, Dartington, 1953.

Foxhole school group. The school was completed in 1932, designed by architect William Leseaze, and closed in 1987.

Re-thatching the Cott Inn. It takes its name from a Dutchman, Jonas Cott, who converted the original cottages into a staging post for shepherds and their flocks on the way into Totnes.

The Cott, photographed c. 1960. On the ancient packhorse route to Ashburton is the long low thatched Cott Inn built in the reign of Edward II and first opened in 1320. In the nineteenth century the Cott combined with adjacent cottages retaining the old, three foot thick walls.

Staverton Bridge built in 1413, together with the Mills, photographed in the 1950s. The river Dart shallows here; the bridge is narrow and strong with bays in which to take refuge. Nowadays the bridge is only wide enough for a single flow of traffic.

Cottages at the scattered settlement of Week, Dartington, c. 1950. Some cottages date back to around the sixteenth and seventeenth century.

Bow Bridge between Ashprington and Tuckenhay. In the 1950s the Waterman's Arms sold petrol and oil.

Cottages in the village of Cornworthy, named for its cereal growing. Photographed here in around 1950.

Broadhempston's Church House Inn around 1960. The Morris 1000s and the Mini van give a clue to the date.

Rattery village, 1956. Situated on the old traveller's road from Kingsbridge to Bristol, Rattery's church and inn date back to the twelfth century.

Dartington Great Hall.
Restored in 1925 by Leonard
and Dorothy Elmhirst.

The reclining stone figure by
Henry Moore in Dartington
Hall Gardens.

127

Eric Morison's plate camera, still in use in the 1960s.

Acknowledgements

Main photographers from the Totnes Image Bank Archive Collection:

Nicholas and Fay Horne
Eric Morison
Rex Gardner
Rosemary Westell
Barrington Weekes

Photographs used in this book from donated images. Contributors who have donated photographs to the Totnes Image Bank and are held on our computer database:

Jeanne Allen
Valerie Belray
Bill Bennett
Phil Bindon
Fred Bridges
Stephen Carter
Margaret Fox
Mrs Harris
Richard Harvey
Mrs Kuyuate

Verity Langford
Margaret Luton
Lewis Major
Chris Mitchell
Val Price
Lilley Ramsden
Jack Woolley
St Mary's church
Totnes Museum

Web-site: www. totnesimagebank.org.uk   Tel: 01803 862183
Totnes Image Bank, Town Mill, Coronation Road, Totnes, Devon TQ9 5DF